fabulous
silkflorals

FOR THE HOME

fabulous silk florals

FOR THE HOME

CELE KAHLE

NORTH LIGHT BOOKS
CINCINNATI. OHIO

www.artistsnetwork.com

about the author

Cele Kahle has been a floral designer for sixteen years, creating floral displays for florists and private clients throughout Ohio. Specializing in silk flower arranging, she currently works as a design consultant, creating custom floral decorations for private homes. A self-taught floral designer herself, Cele loves to share her love of flower arranging with others. She lives with her husband Ken and three children Seth, Stephanie and Hailey in Coldwater, Ohio.

Fabulous Silk Florals for the Home. © 2001 by Cele Kahle. Manufactured in China. All rights reserved. No part of this book may be reproduced in any form or by any electronic or mechanical means including information storage and retrieval systems without permission in writing from the publisher, except by a reviewer, who may quote brief passages in a review. Published by North Light Books, an imprint of F&W Publications, Inc., 4700 East Galbraith Road, Cincinnati, Ohio 45236. (800) 289-0963. First edition.

Other fine North Light Books are available from your local bookstore or art supply store or direct from the publisher.

06 05 04   6 5 4

Library of Congress Cataloging-in-Publication Data

Kahle, Cele,
  Fabulous silk florals for the home / by Cele Kahle.—1st ed.
    p. cm.
  ISBN 1–58180–108–4 (pbk. : alk. paper)
    1. Silk flower arrangement. I. Title

  SB449.3.S44 K34 2001
  745.92—dc21

                          2001016234

Editor: Tricia Waddell
Designer: Stephanie Strang
Production coordinator: John Peavler
Production artist: Lisa Holstein
Photographers: Christine Polomsky and Al Parrish

metric conversion chart

TO CONVERT	TO	MULTIPLY BY
Inches	Centimeters	2.54
Centimeters	Inches	0.4
Feet	Centimeters	30.5
Centimeters	Feet	0.03
Yards	Meters	0.9
Meters	Yards	1.1
Sq. Inches	Sq. Centimeters	6.45
Sq. Centimeters	Sq. Inches	0.16
Sq. Feet	Sq. Meters	0.09
Sq. Meters	Sq. Feet	10.8
Sq. Yards	Sq. Meters	0.8
Sq. Meters	Sq. Yards	1.2
Pounds	Kilograms	0.45
Kilograms	Pounds	2.2
Ounces	Grams	28.4
Grams	Ounces	0.04

acknowledgments

I am extremely thankful to God for blessing me with the gift of creativity so I can share it with others. A special thanks to my husband, Ken, for his love, his patience and always being there for me. His support and encouragement while I was writing this book were invaluable. Many thanks to all of my family and friends who have supported me by asking me to decorate their homes and businesses with my floral designs throughout the years. Thanks to my mom, Cecelia, whom I was named after, for not only passing on her gift of creativity to me, but also for encouraging her sixteen children to work hard. She has always been happy for our successes no matter how big or small. Thank you to my sister Wannitta, whom I first began doing floral designs with, for not only getting me started in the floral designing business but for her constant support and love. Thanks to my sister-in-law Karen, who appreciated me and my talent enough to introduce me to the F&W Publications staff. And to Tricia Waddell, my editor and friend, for the encouragement, guidance and support that made this book possible.

I dedicate this book to my **dedication**

husband, Ken, and children, Seth, Stephanie and Hailey,

because they are my love and my life.

Projects
16

I am so excited to introduce you to a book filled *introduction*

with beautiful flower arrangements that anyone can create and enjoy! When I first

started designing floral arrangements sixteen years ago, I wish I had a book like this one to help me begin my

venture in floral design. I began arranging flowers by looking at a picture of an arrangement I liked and copying

the style while personalizing it with the colors I needed. Learning flower arranging in this way was not easy. I

didn't know the right floral supplies to use or how to use them correctly to make an arrangement look the way

I wanted. Consequently, I had to experiment with different products and ways of doing things, not only wasting

time but money.

When North Light Books approached me, my first thought was there are a million flower-arranging books

out there. But while I was thinking about doing this book, I looked at the various floral books currently available

and found that while there were many books, most had little to no instruction. I then thought of how helpful a

book like this would be for beginners, a book with lots of step-by-step directions and a guide to the range of flo-

ral supplies available. So I wrote this book with that in mind.

In this book you will learn how to do different types of arrangements, swags, topiaries and wreaths. And,

instead of giving you a book filled with photographs of a hundred different types of arrangements, this book gives

you the step-by-step instructions you need so that you can do any arrangement you see and would like to de-

sign on your own. Just try several of the projects featured in this book by following my every step, and you too

will discover your own floral design style in no time.

Getting Started

Learning the basics of floral design will allow you to create silk arrangements to accent any home décor. Whether it's knowing the best silk flowers to choose to brighten up a room or finding the right container to fit your decorating style, this section will tell how to begin designing fabulous floral arrangements for every room in your home.

10

Decorating with Flowers

Open any home decorating magazine and you'll see that interior designers use flowers as a key accessory for every room. Flowers are a sophisticated way to bring the colors, textures, mood and style of a room together, making it warm, personal and inviting. But you don't have to be a professional designer to decorate your home with flowers. The key to creating stunning silk flower arrangements for your home is choosing natural-looking flowers that complement your decorating style. Here are some design tips for creating the perfect floral accents for your home.

FLOWER SELECTION

The best artificial arrangements are made with top-quality, naturalistic flowers. There is a wide range of artificial flowers available, but I believe you get what you pay for. Look for silk flowers that look like their natural counterparts with wired stems, petals and leaves so you can individually bend and reshape each flower to look real. Buy flowers in natural colors; unnaturally colored flowers will make your arrangements look fake. Also, look for flowers that are sturdy so they will withstand handling and look beautiful longer. To find the best-quality silk flowers, comparative shop in craft stores, gift stores and your local florist shops.

COLOR

When choosing colors for a floral arrangement, choose colors that complement or contrast with the colors of the room. To prevent the arrangement from blending in too much, use colors that are slightly darker or lighter than the room colors rather than an exact match. By combining different flower and room colors, you can create interesting contrasts, adding more character to the room. For example, an easy way to brighten up a dark room is by designing an arrangement with light-colored flowers with a few dark accents.

Look around at all the colors present in a room, from the colors of the walls and trim to the range of colors present in draperies and furniture. Pull a few colors from various areas of the room into your floral arrangement. However, be careful not to include too many colors in one arrangement so that it doesn't appear too busy and overwhelming. Instead, select a few accent colors that will visually pull the room together. Also remember that you can pick up room colors in the container you choose, with ribbon accents or by substituting a few dried materials for silk flowers and foliage.

PROPORTION

The best way to determine flowers for an arrangement is by making a bouquet in your hand, and checking the size and color relationship of the flowers. When choosing the size and proportion of the flowers, also consider the size of the container and the style of the décor. I personally chose to use large flowers in the projects throughout the book. Larger flowers give an arrangement a more dramatic look, and they take up more space in the arrange-ment so you will need fewer flowers. Most of the larger flowers are also wired, which allows you to bend and shape them to give a more natural appearance.

In many of the arrangements featured, I use flower stems with multiple blooms per stem. If you cannot find stems with multiple flower blooms, substitute by tap-ing two individual stems together or put the two stems close to one another in the arrangement.

SILK FOLIAGE, BERRIES & FRUIT

Artificial foliage is available in a variety of shapes and colors. Silk greenery is not only available in different shades of green but also in different shades of burgundy, plum and other designer colors, making it a great alternative when you want color without adding more flowers to an arrangement or room. Using realistic-looking foliage can make all the difference in an arrangement, while fake-looking greenery can ruin and cheapen the look of an arrangement. As you will see in the projects, I often mix more than one type of greenery in an arrangement. Mixing greeneries that complement one another is a great way to add color and softness to your arrangement.

Artificial berries and fruit are available in many materials, such as latex, papier-maché, plastic or micro-beaded, each with a distinct look. They are also available in many forms, such as clusters, attached to vines and as individual items. Use them to add color, drama and texture to your arrangements.

CHOOSING CONTAINERS

Containers are as important to the total design as the flowers themselves. When choosing a container, consider the color, texture and size of the arrangement. Also consider where the arrangement will be placed so both the flowers and the container complement your total decorating scheme.

When choosing a container, first consider the style. If you have a country room setting, you might consider using a wicker or wire basket, a terra-cotta pot or a pottery pitcher, for example. If you have a more traditional-style interior, you might consider using an elegant ceramic container or cut glass bowl or vase. Or if contemporary is your style, simple shapes and clean lines with minimal detailing on a ceramic, glass or metallic container are good contemporary accents.

Containers can vary in height or size, depending on their intended use. Low containers are ideal on a dining room table, while taller vases can create a dramatic display behind a sofa or on a pedestal.

LOCATION & PLACEMENT

Choosing the location of an arrangement is critical in deciding its design, color, shape and proportion. To find the best locations for floral decorations, walk through your home and look for places that need color and warmth. Don't forget that arrangements don't always have to be displayed on a table. Swags and wreaths can add interest to a bare wall. Take advantage of tall ceilings by putting an arrangement on top of an armoire or curio cabinet. Accent mirrors, picture frames, mantles or doorways with swags. Place a topiary tree in an empty corner or entryway. Also look at protected outdoor living areas, such as porches, that could be accented with silk wreaths, arrangements or trees. Be creative and experiment with various placement ideas.

STYLE & DESIGN

Matching the design of your arrangement to your room décor is key in creating an integrated look. For example, if you have a country home décor, floral designs that are dense with smaller flowers look great, giving a garden bouquet look to your arrangements. If your home is more traditional, design arrangements with large blooms and spiky flowers for an elegant, airy look. If contemporary is your style, try more free-form arrangements with fewer flowers that feature unusual or dramatic blooms. Also, another way to accessorize a room with flowers is by changing your arrangements seasonally, either by replacing the featured flowers in an arrangement or replacing one or two focal arrangements with new ones. Updating your floral decorations with seasonal flowers, accents and colors is a quick and easy way to give a room a whole new look.

Basic Tools & Techniques

Nothing is more important than having the right tools and materials to create arrangements quickly and easily. Similarly, once you learn basic arranging techniques, you can start creating stunning arrangements like a pro. This section details the basic tools and techniques you need to create any arrangement in this book.

personally prefer sheet foam over the foam blocks because it is more dense and firm, so stems are held more securely.

FLORAL TAPE

Used to wrap stems when using floral picks or to secure flower stems together, floral tape is a self-sealing tape that is activated by the heat from your fingers. While it is available in different shades, I used dark green for all the projects in this book.

FLORAL WIRE

Floral wire comes in different weights or gauges. For the arrangements in this book, you will need 22-gauge wire. Floral wire can be used in many different ways, but I mainly use it to secure bows.

GLITTER FLORAL SPRAY

Glitter floral sprays have bright metallic flecks to brighten and enhance silk flowers and dried materials. These sprays are especially nice for holiday and special occasion arrangements. I use Floralife Perfect Glitter, which is specifically designed for floral materials.

GOLD AEROSOL FLORAL SPRAY

Gold floral spray is wonderful for accenting baskets, dried floral materials, silk flowers and floral accessories. In the projects in this book, I used 24 Karat Gold by Floralife.

HOT GLUE GUN

A hot glue gun can be used for many different projects. I personally like a glue gun that has several heat settings, and I generally use the lowest setting. The low setting

Basic Tools & Supplies

Most craft stores carry the basic flower-arranging tools and materials you will need to create silk arrangements. You can also buy any hard-to-find materials from your local florist. Here are the supplies you will need to complete any arrangement in this book.

CRAFT GLUE

Craft glues such as Tacky Glue are great all-purpose glues that can be used to secure stems into foam.

FLORAL ADHESIVE TAPE

Floral adhesive tapes such as Cling are a sticky claylike material used to secure items in your arrangement. I use floral adhesive tape to attach foam pieces together, secure foam inside a container or

secure a figurine to foam. Cling floral adhesive comes on a roll, so you can pull off pieces to your desired strip lengths.

GREENING PINS

Sometimes called S-pins or floral pins, these pins are used to secure moss or other floral materials to foam.

FLORAL PICKS

Wooden floral picks come in several sizes and are useful in extending stem lengths and securing bows. I use 4" (10cm) floral picks with wire ends on all the arrangements throughout this book.

FLORAL SHEET FOAM

Floral foam is used to secure flower stems in an arrangement. I used 2" (5cm) deep, green foam in all of the projects. I

is hot enough to adhere materials safely. In this book I used a glue gun mainly to secure flowers and fruit picks to wreaths.

PADDLE WIRE

This type of floral wire comes wrapped around a paddle or spool for ease in holding with one hand. Use it to secure and wrap around foam or to make a hanger for a swag.

PLASTIC CANDLE HOLDER

Plastic candle holders come in several sizes to secure a candle safely in an arrangement. The bottom of the holder has a stake so it fits securely in foam.

SERRATED KNIFE

Use a serrated knife to cut floral sheet foam for silk arrangements.

SPRAY FLORAL ADHESIVE

When you need to secure floral materials to a large area, spray floral adhesive works wonders. I often use it to to adhere moss to foam for large arrangements.

WAXED GREEN THREAD

This heavy, green waxed thread comes on a spool. It can be used for securing stems or bows in swags and garlands. Because it is waxed, the thread holds together well without slipping.

WIRE CUTTERS

You need easy-to-handle wire cutters to cut thin silk flower stems or dried material. For heavier stems, a stronger pair may be necessary.

Basic Techniques

These are the basic techniques you will use over and over again to complete the arrangements throughout this book. From stem wrapping to preparing your container, these techniques will make your arrangements look as if they were done by a professional.

PREPARING YOUR CONTAINER WITH FOAM

Depending on the size and shape of your container, there are two ways you can prepare it with foam. The first technique works best for a container that is not very deep and does not have a little ledge around the top. In this technique, and on most of the projects in this book, I stack two pieces of foam. You can stack as many pieces as you need so the foam sits at least 1" (3cm) to 2" (5cm) above the container. To prepare your container using this technique, you need a ruler, greening pins, floral adhesive tape and floral foam.

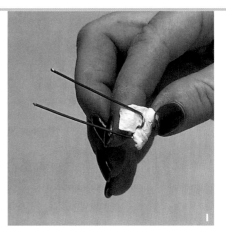

13

> *PREPARING YOUR CONTAINER WITH FOAM: TECHNIQUE 1*
>
> 1 Take a 2" (5cm) strip of floral adhesive tape and wrap it around the top of a greening pin. Do this for several pins based on the diameter of the container opening. For example, if I had a 9" (23cm) diameter container, I would do this to about six greening pins.
>
> 2 Press the greening pins with floral adhesive tape to the bottom of the container. Put a strip of floral adhesive tape in the center of your container. This will make the foam secure inside the container.
>
> 3 Measure the length and width of the base of your container, and cut a piece of foam ½" (1cm) less than these measurements.
>
> 4 Push the foam down firmly into the bowl to meet the greening pins and adhesive at the bottom of the container.

Basic Tools & Techniques *continued*

PREPARING YOUR CONTAINER WITH FOAM:
TECHNIQUE 1 (CONT.)

5 Put two long strips of floral adhesive tape on top of the foam in the container.

6 Measure the top opening of the container, and cut another piece of foam ½" (1cm) smaller to fit the container. Press it down firmly on top of the first piece of foam.

PREPARING YOUR CONTAINER WITH FOAM:
TECHNIQUE 2

The second technique for preparing your container with foam is used when you have a round vase or irregular-shaped container.

1 Press the vase into the foam to make an imprint of the vase opening.

2 Use the imprint as a guide for cutting the foam with a serrated knife. Shave the sides at an angle to fit snugly inside the vase.

3 Put floral adhesive tape around the inside lip of the vase.

4 Press the foam into the vase so it fits snugly, leaving 1½" of foam above the edge of the vase.

14

USING FLORAL PICK EXTENDERS

Wooden floral picks with wire extensions are used for several different reasons: to make a flower stem longer, to make a weak stem stronger and to secure and attach bows. While they come in several different lengths, I generally use the 4" (10cm) size. If the 4" (10cm) size is too long, cut it to the size you prefer. If you need more length than 4" (10cm), purchase floral pick extenders in longer lengths or you can use a wired stem that has been cut from a flower. (A lot of flowers come with extralong stems, so when I cut them off, I keep them in case I need a long extender.) To extend silk flower stems, you need floral tape to securely attach the floral picks with wire extenders. This technique also works for attaching cut wire stems for extralong extenders.

OPENING SILK FLOWERS

When packaged, silk flowers are often folded and flattened. But they can be easily molded and brought to life. Here's an easy way to bring the natural beauty of silk flowers to light.

USING FLORAL PICK EXTENDERS

1 *Take your wooden floral pick with wire and lay it next to your flower stem, extending the pick 1½" (4cm) above the end of the stem. Wrap the wire securely down the stem.*

2 *Begin wrapping the stem with floral tape, starting just above the floral pick extender. Floral tape does not have a right or wrong side. It becomes tacky and adheres to itself as it is stretched and smoothed with your fingers. Hold the flower with one hand and the tape in the other. Begin by stretching and pulling the tape downward. Twist the stem while taping for complete coverage. The tape should be snug, overlapping on its way down the stem.*

3 *Be sure to smooth the tape with your fingers to make it secure. This is how the finished wrapped stem looks.*

OPENING SILK FLOWERS

1 *Most silk flower stems are folded up like this rose stem when you first buy them.*

2 *Begin unfolding the flower from the bottom. Start with the leaves and work your way up the stem. When opening the flowers, arrange the petals as naturally as you can.*

3 *Your silk flower takes on a fresh look when unfolded and molded by your hands. To keep your silk flowers and foliage looking fresh and free of dust, periodically wipe them off with a damp cloth or gently blow-dry the dust off the surface.*

Now that you understand # Projects

the basic techniques of silk flower arranging and

design, it's time to start creating beautiful floral

accents for your home. Throughout the projects

look for designer tips and techniques to help you

create floral decorations like a pro. You'll also find

ideas for project variations so you can customize

each arrangement to your own decorating style.

6 spike stems (2 stems of each color—
I chose sage green, dusty pink and white)

3 fruit pick stems, 24" (61cm) each

1 medium English ivy bush

1 medium grape ivy bush

1 medium frosted maple ivy bush

5 wired or natural curly willow stems

Spanish moss

round ceramic compote, 9" (23cm) diameter,
5" (13cm) tall

green floral sheet foam, 2" (5cm) deep

floral adhesive tape

green floral tape

greening pins

wooden floral picks with wire

Spike & Ivy Arrangement

project 1

This is one of my favorite arrangements because it is so versatile. Place this arrangement on a high piece of furniture, such as a hutch or curio cabinet, or on a low piece of furniture, such as a coffee table or dining table. This arrangement shows the technique of mixing different types of colorful greenery to create color without flowers. This is perfect for a room that already has flowers on the upholstery or draperies but needs a subtle arrangement with some color to visually pull the room together.

20

PREPARE THE CONTAINER
Following the instructions on pages 13–14 for Preparing Your Container With Foam, stack two pieces of floral foam and attach them securely to the container with floral adhesive tape and greening pins. Cover the foam with Spanish moss, and secure it with greening pins.

2 **SEPARATE THE GRAPE IVY**
Cut off three long trailers from the grape ivy bush and set them aside.

3 **INSERT GRAPE IVY BUSH**
Insert the remaining grape ivy bush in the center of the foam.

4 **ADD GRAPE IVY TRAILERS**
Cut the longest trailer to 30" (76cm), and cut two 20" (51cm) trailers. Insert one trailer on either side and one in front. (If you would like the longest trailer to hang over more on one side of a ledge, put the 30" [76cm] one on that side.)

5 **ADD MAPLE IVY**
Cut the maple ivy bush completely apart. Insert the longest stem in the center of the arrangement. Put the rest of the long trailers around the outside, and fill in around the sides with the remaining stems.

6 **ADD ENGLISH IVY**
Cut the English ivy bush apart. Cut four 20" (51cm) stems, one 30" (76cm) stem and a few 15" (38cm) stems. Put the longest trailer on the side where you want more length. With the remaining stems, fill in evenly around the container where there are holes.

22

7

ADD FLOWERS
Cut three spike stems to 28" (71cm) and insert them directly in the center in a triangle formation. Cut three more spike stems to 26" (66cm) and insert them in a triangle around the center spike stems.

9 **CUT FINAL FRUIT PICK**
Using the wire cutters, cut the final 24" (61cm) fruit pick into two pieces.

8 **ADD FRUIT PICKS**
Insert a 24" (61cm) fruit pick on either side of the arrangement. Place them a bit off center.

10 **ADD FINAL FRUIT PICKS**
Add floral pick extenders (see Basic Tools & Techniques, pages 14–15) to the short fruit picks and insert one in the front of the arrangement and one in the back.

11 **ADD WILLOW**
Add five curly willow stems randomly around the arrangement.

12

CREATE VARIATIONS
The spike flowers and willow stems add dimension to this arrangement while keeping it airy so you can still see through it. As a variation, use delphinium or stock for the tall, center flower instead of spike. This arrangement also shows how mixing different types of ivy that complement each other adds interest to an arrangement. Use this technique in other arrangements. For example, mix a simple green ivy with one that has color or is variegated (contains spots or streaks). The mix of ivies will not only add color to a room but look more realistic.

materials:

2 Dendrobium orchid stems

2 freesia stems
(3 stalks of blooms on each stem)

4 delphinium stems

2 lilac stems (3 lilac bunches on each stem)

6 tulips

1 freesia bush (choose a coordinating color—I used a yellow freesia bush with approximately 9 stems)

3 dragon fern stems (2 leaves on each stem)

1 yucca bush or onion grass stems

glass vase, 12" (30cm) tall

glass marbles, enough to fill ¾ of vase

This arrangement is a **Springtime In A Vase**

pleasant welcome, especially after a long, gray winter. By the time March rolls around, I am ready for bright, beautiful blooms of color.

This spring bouquet features popular spring flowers mixed with a tropical flare. Dendrobium orchids and freesia add elegance to this design created in a glass vase with marbles. Anyone can master this arrangement.

No tape, no foam! Just keep playing with the arrangement until you feel the warmth of springtime around you.

1 PREPARE VASE
Make sure your vase is clean, and fill it three-fourths full with marbles. Insert grass or yucca in the center of the vase.

2 ADD ORCHIDS
Cut the orchid stems to 36" (91cm) and insert them in the center of the vase. It is important that you shape these flowers so they look natural. Bend them down to create a flowing effect.

3 ADD FREESIA STEMS
Cut both freesia stems to 31" (79cm) and insert them around the orchids.

4 ADD TULIPS
Cut two tulip stems to 26" (66cm), and insert them in the center of the arrangement. Cut the four remaining tulip stems to 18" (46cm), and insert them around the arrangement angled outward. Bend the flowers so they are facing downward—like a real tulip would when cut and put in a vase.

5 ADD LILACS
Cut both lilac stems to 20" (51cm), and insert them between the shorter tulips.

6 ADD DELPHINIUM
Cut the delphinium stems to 22" (56cm), and insert them in the center of the arrangement.

7

ADD FREESIA BUSH
Cut the freesia bush apart into 20" (51cm) stems, and insert them randomly around the arrangement, filling in the holes, to give the arrangement a uniform but natural look.

8 ***ADD GREENERY***
Cut the dragon fern stems to 18" (46cm), and insert them around the perimeter of the arrangement. If you cannot find dragon fern, substitute a green or variegated ivy.

9 ***CREATE VARIATIONS***
Be creative when picking flowers for your spring bouquet. Notice I used spring flowers with pastel tones. The focal flower in this arrangement is the Dendrobium orchid, so I didn't want to detract from it with too much color. If you want brighter spring shades, try substituting purple irises, yellow daffodils and red tulips, for example, to create a bold, vibrant arrangement.

5 daisy stems (3 to 4 blooms on each stem)

1 small azalea bush

1 geranium bush

1 dusty miller bush

1 begonia bush with trailers

2 plastic curly willow stems with green leaves

3 dragon fern stems (2 leaves on each stem)

green moss

rusted wire wall basket, 22" x 19" x 5" (56cm x 48cm x 13cm)

green floral sheet foam, 2" deep, cut 2 6" x 12" (15cm x 30cm) pieces

paddle wire

floral adhesive tape

green floral tape

greening pins

wooden floral picks with wire

Fill your home with beautiful, # Summer

bright blooms all summer. A rustic wire basket filled with vivid flowers # Patio

makes a beautiful accent for a front porch, patio or sunroom. Brimming # Wall

over with azaleas, geraniums and daisies, this colorful arrangment # Basket

celebrates the brilliant shades of summer and nature

in abundance.

30

1 | PREPARE BASKET
Put two long strips of floral adhesive tape between the two 6" x 12" (15cm x 30cm) pieces of foam. Press the pieces together firmly. Cover the foam on all sides with green moss and secure it with greening pins.

2 | SECURE FOAM TO BASKET
Place the foam inside the wire basket. Using paddle wire, secure the foam by wrapping the wire around the foam and attaching the wire to the back (flat side) of the basket.

3 | INSERT GERANIUM BUSH
Open up the geranium bush, and insert it in the center of the basket.

4 **ADD AZALEAS**
Cut the azalea bush apart. This will allow you to put the flowers closer to the foam and cover a wider area. Insert the azaleas on the right side of the geraniums. By keeping them in the same area, they look more like planted azaleas.

5 **ADD DAISIES**
Cut the daisy stems to 15" (38cm) and insert them mostly on the left side of the arrangement. Mix a couple of stems in and around the azaleas.

6 **ADD DUSTY MILLER**
Cut the dusty miller bush apart, and create four bundles of three stems each. (In the arrangement, these will appear as small dusty miller plants.) Attach a floral pick with wire to each bundle, and wrap the stems and floral pick with green floral tape. This is not only to add length to the bundles but to help secure them and create a sharp end to insert into the floral foam. Insert the dusty miller bundles randomly around the arrangement.

7

ADD GREENERY
Cut the begonia plant apart, and insert five begonia trailers around the perimeter of the arrangement.

8 ***ADD DRAGON FERN***
Insert a stem of dragon fern on the left, front and right sides of the arrangement.

9 ***ADD WILLOW***
Insert two stems of willow in the center of the arrangement, next to the geranium plant toward the back. This particular willow stem had three shoots coming off of it that were three different lengths. You can substitute with natural willow, too.

10

**CREATE
VARIATIONS**
This basket can be
displayed year-round
with a few seasonal
changes. Keep the
greenery in and
replace the summer
flowers with mums
in the fall and tulips
and daffodils in the
spring. For the win-
ter months, add a
new piece of foam
and insert live ever-
green (which stays
green for several
months), a string of
lights and a bow and
you are ready for
the holiday season.

materials:

4 rose stems

2 magnolia stems

3 hydrangea stems

4 larkspur stems
(multiple branches per stem)

2 stems of capensia leaves
(3 branches per stem)

6 eucalyptus branches

3 Holland ivy stems
(or any large-leafed ivy)

2 cone berry branches
(5 to 6 clusters on each branch)

Spanish moss

3 yards (274cm) of 2½" (6cm) wide, sheer
wired ribbon

green floral sheet foam, 2" deep, 4½" x 7"
(11cm x 18cm)

cardboard, 4½" x 7" (11cm x 18cm)

paddle wire

green floral tape

greening pins

wooden floral picks with wire

hot glue gun

This versatile swag design # Hydrangea Swag

This versatile swag design can be made over and over again with different flowers and displayed in various places throughout your home. Hang it over a doorway, mirror or framed picture to add color and texture to a wall. Or omit the hanger and use this swag on a dining table with candlesticks on either side to create a stunning centerpiece.

project 4

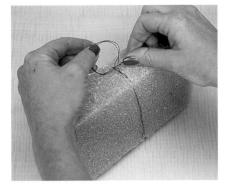

4 PREPARE GREENERY
Cut two 20" (51cm) and two 12" (30cm) capensia stems. Capensia leaves are usually used to make silk ficus or capensia trees. I use them a lot for background greenery in swags or one-sided arrangements.

36

1 CREATE WIRE HANGER
Measure a 6" (15cm) lead of paddle wire, then begin wrapping the paddle wire securely around the foam block twice, leaving 6" (15cm) of wire at the end. Take the two end wires and twist them together to make a loop on the back of the foam for a hanger.

2 ATTACH CARDBOARD BACKING
Using the glue gun, glue the cardboard to the back of the foam. The backing will protect your wall or table from foam scratches.

5 ADD CAPENSIA STEMS
Insert the two longest capensia stems horizontally on the left and right sides of the foam so the arrangement is around 3' (91cm) across. Insert the two shorter capensia stems on the top and bottom of the foam.

6 ADD ROSES
Cut two 18" (46cm) and two 10" (25cm) rose stems. Insert the two long stems on the left and right sides of the foam block on top of the capensia leaves. Insert the two shorter stems on the top and bottom, but angle these roses a little off center from the capensia stems at a diagonal.

3 ADD MOSS
Cover the front and sides of the foam with Spanish moss, and secure it with greening pins.

7 **ADD SIDE HYDRANGEAS**
Cut two 13" (33cm) stems of hydrangea, and insert them on the left and right sides of the foam block. Position the stems on top of the roses but a little off to the side to avoid blocking the roses.

8 **ADD CENTER HYDRANGEA**
Cut one 7" (18cm) hydrangea, and insert it in the front center of the foam block. Insert the extra hydrangea leaves around the center hydrangea.

9 **ADD MAGNOLIAS**
Cut two magnolia stems to 11" (28cm), and insert them on the left and right sides of the floral foam near the center hydrangea.

10

ADD CONE BERRY
Cut two 24"(61cm) and two 12" (30cm) cone berry stems. Insert the two long stems on the left and right sides of the foam between the hydrangeas and the roses. Insert the two shorter stems on the top and bottom of the foam block at a diagonal to the center hydrangea.

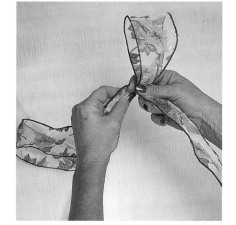

11 **MAKE BOW TUCKS**
Cut two 23" (58cm) lengths of ribbon. Leaving a 6" (15cm) streamer, make a loop and twist the ribbon.

12 **ADD LOOPS**
Make another loop the same size as the first loop, and twist. Repeat this step until you have three loops of the same size. Cut the ribbon, leaving another 6" (15cm) streamer. Secure the bow in the center with a wired floral pick. Repeat steps 11 and 12 to complete a second bow.

13 **INSERT BOWS**
Insert the bows on either side of the center hydrangea. Fluff the bows out, and have a bow streamer facing to the side top and the side bottom of the swag.

14 **ADD LARKSPUR**
Cut two 24" (61cm) and two 16" (41cm) larkspur stems. Insert the two longer stems on the left and right sides of the foam block under the cone berries. Insert the two shorter stems on the top and bottom of the foam on a diagonal from the cone berries.

15 **ADD EUCALYPTUS**
Cut two 24" (61cm) eucalyptus stems, and insert them on the left and right sides under the hydrangeas. Cut four 16" (41cm) eucalyptus stems, and insert one on either side of the longer eucalyptus stems.

16 ***ADD FINAL EUCALYPTUS***
Cut eight 12" (30cm) eucalyptus stems, and insert them in a circle around the center hydrangea.

17 ***ADD HOLLAND IVY***
Cut eight large Holland ivy leaves, and add wired floral pick extenders. (See Basic Techniques, page 15.) Insert the ivy around the base of the arrangement on the sides. Cut two small leaves of Holland ivy and add extenders. Insert the small leaves around the center hydrangea on a diagonal.

18 ***POSITION FLOWERS***
In a swag arrangement, the flowers are layered on top of each other. Make sure you are not covering up any flowers so all the blooms are visible. Adjust the blooms so they face more toward you. If you took any flower out of the foam several times to reposition it and the flower feels loose, glue the stem in with craft glue so it doesn't fall out when hung. If you want a larger swag, just use larger flowers. If you use too many small flowers in a large swag, it will have a cluttered look.

materials:

3 hydrangea stems

3 magnolia stems

3 tea rose stems

4 larkspur stems (multi-stemmed)

3 cone berry stems

12 eucalyptus stems

1 small green variegated ivy bush

Spanish moss

faux stone vase

floral sheet foam, 2" (5cm) deep

floral adhesive tape

green floral tape

greening pins

wooden floral picks with wire

41

This basic floral design can

Hydrangea & Magnolia Centerpiece

be used to create many arrangements for your

home. Designed to coordinate with the hydrangea

swag on page 34, this elegant table arrangement is

made to be viewed from all sides. It features large, sumptuous blooms, perfect

for a room that needs a dramatic focal point.

42

1 PREPARE CONTAINER
To fill your container with floral foam, refer to the basic technique, Preparing Your Container With Foam, on pages 13–14. Cover the foam with Spanish moss, and secure with greening pins.

2 PREPARE HYDRANGEAS
Cut the hydrangea stems into three sections as shown. The flower head stem should be approximately 6" (15cm).

3 INSERT HYDRANGEAS
Insert the hydrangea blossoms in a triangular formation, and angle them outward. Insert the remaining hydrangea greenery stems around the blossoms.

4 ADD MAGNOLIAS
Cut the magnolia stems to 15" (38cm). Insert the stems in a triangle formation in the center of the arrangement, between and above the hydrangeas.

5 ADD ROSES
Cut the rose stems to 10" (25cm). Insert the stems between the hydrangeas at an angle, extending beyond the hydrangeas.

6 ADD LARKSPUR
Cut one stem of larkspur to 26" (66cm), and insert it directly in the center of the arrangement. Cut the remaining three stems of larkspur to 16" (41cm), and insert them in a triangle formation between the magnolias.

7 ADD CONE BERRIES

Cut one cone berry stem to 26" (66cm), and insert it in the center of the arrangement next to the center larkspur stem. Cut the remaining cone berry stems to approximately 12" (30cm), and insert them next to the roses.

8 ADD EUCALYPTUS

Cut one stem of eucalyptus to 28" (71cm), three stems to 20" (51cm) and eight stems to 10" (25cm). Insert the tallest stem in the center of the arrangement. Insert the three 20" (51cm) stems near the larkspur in the center of the arrangement, and stagger the remaining eucalyptus around the bottom of the arrangement. Insert one above each rose and one beside each rose. Add floral pick extenders if necessary.

9 ADD IVY

Cut six ivy stems to 11" to 12" (28cm to 30cm), and insert them around the base of the arrangement so they trail over the sides. Bend the ivy stems slightly so they create a flowing effect.

10 CREATE VARIATIONS

I like to use large flowers in arrangements like this one because large blooms take up more space and give an arrangement a less cluttered look. And while larger flowers are more expensive, you will use fewer flowers to complete your design. To create variations on this arrangement replace the magnolias, roses and hydrangeas with other large blooms such as lilies, dahlias or sunflowers.

materials:

1 frosted grape ivy bush

2 spider plant bushes

2 small wandering Jew bushes (tradescantia bushes)

5 curly willow stems (I used wired, you can use natural also)

Spanish moss

oval basket, 10" x 16" (25cm x 41cm), 7" (18cm) deep

green floral sheet foam, 2" (5cm) deep

floral adhesive tape

green floral tape

greening pins

wooden floral picks with wire

Mixed Greenery Arrangement

project 6

Greenery adds so much warmth and color to a home, I don't believe you can have too much of it. This simple arrangement can be displayed in many places in the home, especially near patterned furniture or draperies where a simple arrangement looks best. Mix plain greenery with foliage that has colors that match your décor. When you mix different types of greenery that complement one another, it softens the arrangement and the greenery looks more realistic.

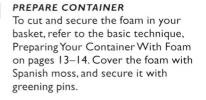

46

1 PREPARE CONTAINER
To cut and secure the foam in your basket, refer to the basic technique, Preparing Your Container With Foam on pages 13–14. Cover the foam with Spanish moss, and secure it with greening pins.

2 INSERT SPIDER PLANTS
Insert the two spider plants in the center of the foam side by side.

3 ADD WANDERING JEW
Insert one wandering Jew plant left of center in front of the spider plants.

5 ADD FROSTED GRAPE IVY
Cut all the stems of the frosted grape ivy bush apart. Add wooden floral pick extenders to the shorter stems. Insert the short stems around the outer edges of the arrangement to fill in around the spider plants.

4 ADD SECOND WANDERING JEW BUSH
Cut off the longest trailing stem of the second wandering Jew bush and set it aside. Insert the bush in the back of the spider plants, right of center. Put the remaining wandering Jew stem in the center of the spider plants toward the front.

6 **ADD FROSTED GRAPE IVY TRAILERS**
Insert the long, trailing ivy stems on the sides of the arrangement where you want them to trail over the basket.

7 **ADD WILLOW**
Add a few curly willow branches randomly as desired.

8
CREATE VARIATIONS
If you want to design variations on this arrangement, the trick is to be creative in mixing your greenery. Hold different greens side by side to see if they blend together nicely. You can omit the willow branches if you don't need the height, or keep them in for added interest.

materials:

2 gold-tipped tiger lily stems
(multiple blooms per stem)
3 gold-tipped rose stems
3 gold-tipped delphinium stems
3 gold-tipped hydrangea stems
gold curly ting ting
gold leaf ivy
green moss

gilded vase, 11"(28cm) tall
green floral sheet foam, 2" (5cm) deep
floral adhesive tape
green floral tape
greening pins
wooden floral picks with wire

This striking one-sided arrangement is **Horn O' Plenty Arrangement** highly versatile because you can creatively arrange the flowers off center with unique style and flair.

Featuring the deep jewel tones of autumn and large, dramatic blooms, this arrangement makes an elegant centerpiece. One-sided arrangements such as this one are perfect on pieces of furniture that are sitting against a wall.

project 7

50

1 SHAPE FLORAL FOAM
When you need to cut foam to fit inside an irregular-shaped vase, press the vase into the foam to make an imprint. Use the imprint as a guide for cutting the foam to fit inside the vase.

2 CUT AND SECURE FOAM
Use a knife to cut the foam, and then shave the sides to fit. Put floral adhesive tape around the inside lip of the vase. Press the foam into the vase so it fits snugly, leaving 1½" (4cm) of foam above the edge of the vase.

3 ADD MOSS
Cover the foam with moss, and secure it with greening pins.

4 ADD DELPHINIUM STEMS
Cut the delphinium stems to 20" (51cm), 17" (43cm) and 15" (38cm). Add the three stems of delphinium to the center of the arrangement in a triangle shape. These will be your tallest flowers.

5 **ADD HYDRANGEAS**
Cut the hydrangea stems to 6" (15cm), 8" (20cm) and 13" (33cm). Insert them in a triangle shape, placing the tallest stem left of center.

6 **ADD ROSES**
Cut two rose stems to 10" (25cm) and one stem to 8" (20cm). Save the extra rose leaves on their stems. Insert the long roses on either side of the arrangement. Insert the shorter rose above the center hydrangea. Angle all the rose stems upward as shown.

7 **ADD LILIES**
Cut the tiger lilies to 12" (30cm) each and insert one stem on each side of the arrangement. Angle one lily stem toward the back and one toward the front of the arrangement.

52

8 ADD ROSE LEAVES
Add wooden floral pick extenders to the extra rose stems with leaves. (See Basic Tools & Techniques, page 15.) Fill in any holes in the arrangement.

9 ADD IVY
Cut two 20" (51cm) ivy stems and two 15" (38cm) ivy stems. Insert the ivy around the base of the arrangement with the longer ivy stems to the side toward the back.

10 PREPARE CURLY TING TING
Using green floral tape, tape three 24" to 26" (61cm to 66cm) stems of curly ting ting together.

tip: Curly ting ting comes in many colors, but if you can't find the color you want, just spray it with floral spray paint to change the color.

11 ADD CURLY TING TING
Insert the taped bundle of curly ting ting in the center of the arrangement between the delphinium stems. Add four more single strands of curly ting ting in various lengths in a diamond shape around the arrangement.

12

CREATE VARIATIONS

To create variations on this arrangement, remember that larger flower blooms usually work best used in the center of a one-sided arrangement. The center flowers are the focal point of the arrangement, so pick flowers that are unique and accent your room. Use wired flowers because they have more body and can be shaped more naturally. Also, if you are using a tall container, bend the flowers that come out around the vase in an upward position so you can view them easily and create a flowing effect.

materials:

4 hydrangea stems with thick, hand-wrapped stems

2 micro-beaded fruit picks

flocked Holland ivy

small leaf, green English ivy

button leaf ivy

green moss

4 yards (366cm) of 1½" (4cm) wide sheer wired ribbon

faux stone vase, 8" (20cm) tall

gold floral spray paint

22-gauge floral wire

green floral sheet foam, 2" (5cm) deep

floral adhesive tape

green floral tape

greening pins

wooden floral picks with wire

small plastic bag

This spectacular topiary # Hydrangea Topiary

can be designed with any large flower that has a sturdy hand-wrapped stem. Place this arrangement anywhere you

project 8

want a touch of Victorian romance. Add the decorative ribbon and micro-beaded fruit to give that extra sparkle and elegance.

56

ADD GOLD ACCENTS TO CONTAINER

This particular stone container is ivory with brown veins throughout. Since I am using gold accents in the arrangement, I wanted to add a little of that to the container. Take a small plastic bag and scrunch it in one hand. Spray a small amount of gold floral spray on the bag, and lightly sponge it on the container.

2 PREPARE CONTAINER

Refer to the Basic Techniques section on Preparing Your Container With Foam, pages 13–14. Follow these directions to fill your container with floral foam. Cover the foam with moss and secure it with greening pins.

3 PREPARE HYDRANGEAS

Cut the four hydrangea stems to 21" (53cm). Open up each hydrangea, and snip the bottom leaf off the stem. Save the leaves for later use.

4 ADD GREENERY TO HYDRANGEAS

Cut a 12" (30cm) stem of green ivy. Use floral tape to attach the cut hydrangea leaf and ivy stem to a hydrangea stem 1" (3cm) from the base of the blossoms. Wrap the floral tape around the stems several times to make sure it is secure. Repeat this step for all four hydrangea stems.

5 **ARRANGE HYDRANGEA BUNCHES**
Bend the ivy downward in a flowing position, and fluff the hydrangeas so they are nicely rounded.

6 **ADD IVY TO HYDRANGEAS**
Cut two large Holland ivy leaves from the stem and cut a 10" (25cm) stem of button leaf ivy. Using green floral tape, tape the Holland ivy and button leaf on the hydrangea stem in the same place as specified in step 4. Repeat this step to make a total of four hydrangea bunches.

7 **CREATE TOPIARY FORM**
Group three hydrangea bunches in a cluster. Place the fourth hydrangea bunch in the center, raised 1" (3cm) above the other three bunches. Tape all four bunches together securely with floral tape in the same spot where the greenery was taped on the hydrangea stems.

8 INSERT TOPIARY INTO FOAM
Push the hydrangea stems into the center of the container. Adjust the hydrangeas to the desired height.

tip: If the hydrangea stems feel loose in the foam, hot glue them in to secure them.

58

9 START BOWS
To create the bows, cut the ribbons into two 1½-yard (137cm) strips and one yard-long (91cm) strip. With the first 1½-yard (137cm) ribbon, leave a 3" (8cm) streamer, then make a loop and twist the ribbon in the center.

10 COMPLETE BOW
Make a total of four loops, twisting each loop in the center before creating the next loop. Secure the bow in the center with a 4" (10cm) piece of floral wire. Repeat steps 9 and 10 to create a second bow with the other 1½-yard (137cm) ribbon.

11 ATTACH BOWS
Use the floral wire on the bows to attach one bow on a hydrangea bunch toward the front right side and one bow on the left back side of the topiary. Cut off any excess wire, and hide the ends inside the topiary ball.

12 ATTACH STREAMER
Cut the leftover yard of ribbon into a 2' (61cm) strip and a 1' (30cm) strip. Attach the 2' (61cm) ribbon to the topiary stems at the base of the ball with a 3" (8cm) piece of floral wire. Cut off any excess wire, and hide the ends inside the topiary ball.

13 SPIRAL STREAMER
Spiral the ribbon all the way down and around the topiary stems. Add a wooden floral pick extender 4" (10cm) from the end of the ribbon. Secure the ribbon with the floral pick in the floral foam at the base of the stems.

15
ADD GREENERY
Cut a 14" (36cm) stem of English ivy, and weave it in and around the topiary stems. Begin spiraling under the topiary ball and wind down the stems. Insert the stem end in the floral foam. (You may have to add a floral pick extender if the stem does not have a sharp end to insert in the foam.)

14 ADD RIBBON TAIL
Attach a wooden floral pick extender to the end of the 1' (30cm) ribbon, and insert it into the floral foam opposite the first steamer, next to the topiary stems. Cut the ribbon to the desired length.

16 ADD BEADED FRUIT
Cut the beaded fruit stems to 4" (10cm). Insert them into the floral foam on a diagonal opposite from each other near the topiary stems.

17 **ADD HOLLAND IVY**
Cut three large Holland ivy leaves, and add wooden floral pick extenders. Insert the leaves around the topiary stems.

18 **ADD BUTTON LEAF AND ENGLISH IVY**
Cut three 10" (25cm) button leaf ivy stems. Insert them into the floral foam in a triangle pattern, and arrange them to flow over the edge of the container. Cut three 10" (25cm) stems of English ivy. Insert the English ivy stems in the floral foam in between the button ivy, filling in any holes.

19 **CREATE VARIATIONS**
If you cannot find Holland ivy or button leaf ivy, substitute other ivy varieties. Choose ivies that blend together nicely and complement the flowers you are using. Add more ivy if you want a fuller arrangement.

materials:

3 rose stems

4 double-stemmed prunis
(or any small spiky flowers)

2 micro-beaded fruit picks

2 micro-beaded grape picks

1 small frosted grape ivy bush
with bittersweet

1 small English ivy bush

medium twig wreath, 36" (91cm)

1 yard (91cm) of 1½" (4cm) wide
sheer ribbon

wooden floral picks with wire

hot glue gun

This twig wreath has a country flair, but Twig
Wreath
when you add the beaded fruit, you suddenly have an elegant

wreath that will add charm to any décor. Finish it off *project 9*

with sheer decorative ribbon accents, and display it on a wall or door, inside or out.

64

1 **ATTACH FROSTED GRAPE IVY**
Cut four 10" (25cm) stems of frosted grape ivy, and hot glue them in the inner circle of the wreath.

tip: If you cannot find ivy with berries attached, buy the berries on a stem and glue them in with the ivy.

2 **ADD BEADED FRUIT**
Cut the fruit picks to 8" (20cm). Hot glue them opposite each other in the inner circle of the wreath.

3 **ADD BEADED GRAPES**
Cut the two grape picks to 8" (20cm). Hot glue them opposite each other between the beaded fruit picks in the inner circle of the wreath.

4 **ADD ROSES**
Cut the rose stems to 6" (15cm). Hot glue them in the inner circle of the wreath in a triangle formation.

5 **ADD PRUNIS**
Cut four double stems of prunis to 8" to 10" (20cm to 25cm). Glue them around the inner circle of the wreath, and curve the stems inward.

6 **ADD ENGLISH IVY**
Cut the English ivy bush apart and cut nine stems from 6" to 10" (15cm to 25cm). Glue four shorter stems around the inner circle of the wreath. Glue five of the longer stems around the perimeter of the wreath, and curve the stems to flow with the twigs.

7 **MAKE BOW TUCK**
Cut the sheer ribbon into thirds. Begin the bow tucks by pinching the ribbon between your fingers approximately 4" (10cm) from the end of the ribbon. The endpiece of ribbon will become the first streamer of the bow. Twist the ribbon with your fingers and form a small hoop. Make another loop, leaving a 4" (10cm) piece of ribbon for another streamer.

8 **SECURE BOW**
To secure your bow tuck, attach it to a wooden floral pick by wrapping it with the wire. Wrap the excess wire down the floral pick. Cut the floral pick to 3" (8cm). Follow steps 7 and 8 to make a total of three bow tucks.

9 **ADD BOW TUCKS**
Insert the three bows between the roses, and secure them with hot glue.

10 **CREATE VARIATIONS**
If you want to turn this into a holiday wreath, just spray the twig wreath base with gold floral spray paint. Add some evergreen that is glittered with gold, holiday flowers, fruit picks and a bow, and you'll have a festive wreath for the holiday season.

materials:

weighted double-ball topiary form,
50" (127cm) tall, with a 12" (30cm)
diameter ball and 10" (25cm) diameter ball

2 large grape ivy bushes with grapes

2 large frosted grape ivy bushes

3 amaranthus stems

green moss

willow branches

polyresin pot, 24" (61cm) tall

floral spray adhesive

greening pins

craft glue

This elegant topiary tree looks spectacular Ivy Topiary Tree

placed in an empty corner next to a piece of furniture or on a front porch. The design features grape ivy with red and purple grapes for color, making it perfect for a dining or kitchen area.

project 10

There are many beautiful silk greenery bushes available in different colors and textures, so you can customize this tree to your décor. Add a little evergreen and string lights and you can dress up this topiary tree for the holidays, too!

PLACE FORM IN CONTAINER
Insert the topiary form in the container, and cover the base with green moss. Secure the moss with greening pins.

2 ### APPLY MOSS
Spray the floral spray adhesive onto small sections of the topiary balls, and apply the moss to the foam.

3 ### ADD GREENING PINS
Use greening pins if necessary to secure the moss on the topiary balls.

4 ### ADD IVY TRAILERS
Cut off the long ivy trailer stems from all the ivy bushes and wind them around the topiary balls. Use greening pins to secure the trailers. Crisscross the two different types of ivy over each other.

5 ### FILL IN WITH SHORT IVY STEMS
Cut 6" (15cm) stems of the different ivy bushes. Insert the stems in around the long trailers to fill in the gaps and holes.

6 ### GLUE IVY STEMS
Using craft glue, glue the short ivy stems into the topiary foam if you plan to place the topiary outdoors.

7

FILL IN CONTAINER
Insert varying lengths of ivy stems into the base of the topiary to trail over the container. Fill in any gaps or holes with short ivy stems.

8 **ADD AMARANTHUS**
Add one stem of amaranthus to each topiary ball and the base. Stagger the stem placement as shown.

9 **ADD WILLOW**
If desired, insert willow branches randomly throughout the topiary.

10 **CREATE VARIATIONS**
If you cannot find a premade topiary form to create this project, try making your own. Get a 2" (5cm) diameter dowel rod, and paint it brown. Insert the rod through a 12" (30cm) and halfway into a 10" (25cm) diameter green foam ball, leaving approximately 15" (38cm) between the balls. Fill the container with stacks of floral foam and glue the rod into the foam to hold it securely.

materials:

4 sunflower stems (3 blooms per stem)

1 wired bittersweet stem, 30" (76cm) long

4 wired curly willow stems

6 medium foam gourds (assorted)

1 small green/cream variegated ivy bush

3 fruit picks

preserved or silk fall leaves

Spanish moss

round metal bowl, 8½" (22cm) diameter

green floral sheet foam, 2" (5cm) deep

floral adhesive tape

green floral tape

greening pins

wooden floral picks with wire

hot glue gun

Showcase the vivid colors of autumn in your Fall home with this fall-themed table arrangement. This design Harvest features bright gourds, fruit, bittersweet, autumn Centerpiece leaves and sunflowers. Bring the outdoors in by including *project* a broad range of silk plant materials in your arrangements. It's a great alternative to an all-flower arrangement, and it provides lots of interesting colors and textures.

72

1 **PREPARE CONTAINER**
Refer to the basic technique, Preparing Your Container With Foam, on pages 13–14 for directions on cutting and filling your container with floral foam. Cover the foam with Spanish moss, and use greening pins to secure the moss to the foam.

2 **INSERT PERIMETER SUNFLOWERS**
Cut six sunflower stems to 15" (38cm). Insert the sunflowers in a circle around the base of the arrangement.

3 **ADD CENTER SUNFLOWERS**
Cut three more sunflowers with 6" (15cm) stems and one with a 12" (30cm) stem. Insert the tallest stem into the center of the arrangement. Insert the two shorter stems in front of the tall stem to create a triangle pattern.

4 **ADD FRUIT**
Cut two fruit picks to 8" (20cm) and one to 11" (28cm). Insert the tallest stem in the center of the foam in front of the tallest sunflower. Insert the two shorter stems to the right and left of the center fruit pick to create a triangle.

5 **PREPARE GOURDS**
Poke a small hole in each foam gourd with a knife.

tip: You may have plastic gourds that come with a floral pick on them already. If so, just skip steps 5 and 6 and go on to step 7.

6 **ADD FLORAL PICKS TO GOURDS**
Cut the wires off the floral picks. Using a glue gun, glue a floral pick inside the hole of each gourd.

7
INSERT GOURDS
Insert the gourds randomly throughout the arrangement.

8

ADD IVY

Cut two ivy stems to 20" (51cm) and insert them on the right and left sides of the arrangement. Fill in the arrangement with shorter stems of ivy of various lengths. Bend the ivy to give it a more natural, flowing look.

9 ***ADD FALL LEAVES***

Insert the leaves around the bottom of the arrangement between the fruit and gourds. If you are using preserved fall leaves instead of silk, add wooden floral picks to the stems for support.

10 ***ADD BITTERSWEET***

Add a floral pick extender to the thinner top end of a stem of bittersweet. Curve the bittersweet around the arrangement in a half circle about 2" (5cm) above the tallest sunflower to create a caged effect.

11 ADD CURLY WILLOW
In this particular arrangement, wired willow is needed because it has to bend. Cut three stems of wired curly willow to 40" (102cm) each. Add floral picks to the thinner ends, and form a cage around the arrangement. Cut one stem of willow in half, and make two smaller half circles around the arrangement.

12 CREATE VARIATIONS
If you have access to real gourds, they work great in this arrangement, too. But don't forget to take them out of the arrangement before you store it because they will eventually mold.

materials:

2 magnolia stems
1 rose stem
4 gold ivy stems
2 sugar crab apple stems (or berry stems)
gold dust baby's breath

3 yards (274cm) of 1½" (4cm)
or 2" (5cm) wide sheer wired ribbon
waxed green thread (or paddle wire)
green floral tape

This type of swag is very **Hand-Tied**

easy to assemble and can be used in so many different ways. Design **Rose**

this swag with any flowers you might have left over from a previous **Swag**

arrangement. Display it above a picture or mirror, on

a shelf with a figurine or candlestick, on a door or just sitting on a table curved

around a lamp. The list of creative placement ideas is endless. It is amazing how

little accent pieces like this swag can tie a whole room together.

78

1 GATHER STEMS
Gather a bouquet of stems starting with the crab apple on the bottom. Weave a 24" (61cm) stem of gold ivy and a 14" (36cm) ivy stem within the crab apple stem. Add a magnolia on top, and hold it in a bundle.

2 SECURE STEMS
Wrap the stems securely with green floral tape.

3 ADD BABY'S BREATH
Add several long stems and a few shorter stems of baby's breath behind and around the magnolia stem, and tape it to the stems.

4 CUT STEMS
Cut stems to about 4" (10cm) from the magnolia bloom.

5 SECURE BUNCHES TOGETHER
Repeat steps 1 through 4 to create a second bundle. Lay the bundles facing opposite each other, and cross the stems in the center, leaving 4" (10cm) of stem showing. Tie the stems together securely in several places with the waxed thread or paddle wire.

6 TAPE SWAG TOGETHER
After tying the bundles together, wrap the stems with floral tape in the center to secure the stems and give a finished look.

7 ADD ROSE

Cut the rose stem to 6" (15cm). Bend the stem to the side so the rose is facing up. Using waxed thread or paddle wire, secure the rose in the center of the swag where the stems have been taped. Cut off the rose leaves and tie them in with waxed thread or paddle wire near the rose blossom.

8 MAKE BOW

Make a four-loop ribbon bow with four streamers following the technique on pages 83–84. Position the bow in the center of the swag.

9 ADD BOW

Secure the bow by tying it to the stems with two of the streamers on the back of the taped stems. Center the rose between the bow with two loops on either side of it. Cut the ends of the streamers into a V-cut.

10 CREATE VARIATIONS

Be creative when making your own variations on this swag. Substitute hydrangeas, gardenias or lilies for the roses, try Queen Anne's lace instead of baby's breath or eucalyptus instead of ivy. For a holiday look, try this swag using poinsettias.

materials:

1 magnolia spray, 30" (76cm) stem
(1 large bloom, 2 medium blooms
and 2 small bud blooms)

1 single magnolia stem

2 blackberry sprays

1 rose with berries spray, 12" (30cm)

frosted grape ivy

3 gold bell cups

7 gold twigs

6 yards (549cm) of 3" (8cm)
wide wired ribbon

35-light strand of holiday lights

36" (91cm) wide pine and cedar wreath
with pine cones

gold floral spray paint

gold glitter floral spray

22-gauge floral wire

wooden floral picks with wire

hot glue gun

A pine wreath with # Wintergreen Wreath

gold and glitter accents looks beautiful on any wall, above a

fireplace or on a door. This wreath features magnolias

and roses, so it is not limited to just the holidays but can be enjoyed throughout

the winter months.

1 **OPEN WREATH**
When you purchase a wreath, it usually comes smashed and flat. Open the wreath up by stretching some pine stems to the side and some straight up so it looks full and natural.

2 **CREATE GOLD ACCENTS**
Lightly spray the wreath with gold spray paint to create gold accents. Spray the pine cones a little more heavily with gold spray to make them stand out.

3 **ADD MAGNOLIA SPRAY**
Attach the magnolia spray to one side of the wreath, and secure it with the wreath branches by twisting them around the center of the magnolia stems. Open the magnolia spray and curve it to lie on top of the wreath.

4 **ADD SINGLE-STEM MAGNOLIA**
Cut the single magnolia stem to 5" (13cm) and hot glue it in place toward the bottom right side of the wreath opposite the magnolia spray.

5
ADD ROSES
Cut the rose spray in half to create two 6" (15cm) stems. Insert the stems on either side of the large magnolia at a diagonal. Use the glue gun to secure the stems.

6 **START BOW**
Cut 2 yards (183cm) of ribbon to create the bow. Begin by pinching the ribbon to make a small center loop.

7 **ADD LOOPS**
Twist the ribbon in the center, and make a large loop. Continue making loops until you have four loops, the final two loops being a little larger than the first two. Remember to twist the ribbon after you make each loop.

8 **ADD STREAMERS**
Cut a 36" (91cm) length of ribbon for the streamers. Fold the ribbon in half to find the center, and add the ribbon to the bow so you have two streamers.

9

SECURE BOW
Secure the bow
and steamers by
wrapping them
together with floral
wire in the center
of the bow.

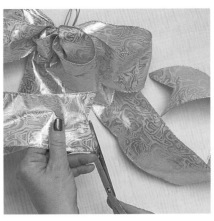

10

TRIM STREAMERS
Finish the ends of
the streamers with
a V-cut.

84

11

ADD BOW
Insert the bow
underneath the
large magnolia. Use
the floral wire in
the center of the
bow to secure the
bow to the wreath.

12 **MAKE BOW TUCKS**
Create a bow tuck with 14" (36cm)
of ribbon by first making a large
loop. Attach the ends of the ribbon
to a floral pick by wrapping the wire
to secure the ribbon ends together.

13 **INSERT BOW TUCK**
Insert the bow tuck opposite the bow on the other side of
the large magnolia. Secure it in place with your glue gun.

tip: You can add as many bow tucks as you like if you want your
bow to appear fuller.

14 **ADD STREAMER**

Cut a 10" (25cm) piece of ribbon, and attach it to a floral pick with the wire extender. Cut a V-cut in the other end of the ribbon, and insert it on the perimeter side of the single magnolia. Secure it with the glue gun. Bring one of the long streamers from the bow made earlier and secure the end under the magnolia using the glue gun.

15 **ADD IVY**

Cut three stems of ivy to 12" (30cm), 16" (41cm) and 24" (61cm). Insert and glue in the longest stem underneath the large magnolia and angle it down. Insert and glue in the 12" (30cm) stem to the side of the large center magnolia. Insert and glue in the 16" (41cm) stem above the center magnolia.

16 **ADD BLACKBERRIES**

Cut the blackberry sprays to 24" (61cm). Insert them diagonally across from each other on top of the ivy. Secure the stems in place with your hot glue gun.

86

17 ADD BELL CUPS
Cut two bell cup stems to 6" (15cm) and one to 12" (30cm). Insert the two shorter stems diagonally across from each other on either side of the large magnolia as shown, and secure with the hot glue gun. Insert the longest bell cup off center along the longest ivy stem pointing downward. Secure it in place with the glue gun.

18 ADD GOLD TWIGS
Cut the gold twig branches to various lengths between 6" (15cm) and 20" (51cm). Place them randomly around the wreath, and secure them in place with the glue gun.

tip: If you cannot find gold twigs, just spray natural twigs with gold spray paint.

19 ADD GLITTER
Spray the entire wreath with gold glitter spray.

20 ADD HOLIDAY LIGHTS
Weave holiday lights throughout the wreath. Turn the lights on, and watch all the gold accents in the wreath glisten and sparkle!

21

***CREATE
VARIATIONS***
Since this wreath
features flowers
that are not holi-
day specific, you
can display this
wreath through-
out the winter
from November
to February. To
customize it more
for the holiday
season, use poin-
settia as the fea-
tured flower.

project
Wintergreen Holiday Swag

Make a swag to coordinate with your holiday wreath. Quick and easy to make, all
you need are two pine sprays with cones
and two rose stems with berries like the
ones used in the wreath. Lightly spray the
pine with gold spray paint. (I spray the
pine cones a little heavier so they are
more solid gold.) Lay the pine sprays end
to end, crossing the stems. Tie the stems
together using green waxed thread or
paddle wire. Lay the rose stems on top of
the pine sprays, and secure the stems with
waxed thread or paddle wire. Hide the
rose stems under the pine greens. Make a
6-loop bow with 8" (20cm) streamers, and
attach it to the center of the swag using
the floral wire on the bow. And, for that
extra touch, weave a 20-strand set of
lights within the swag. You can display the
swag by hanging it vertically or horizontally on a wall, as a table centerpiece by setting it in a small sleigh or open box with a
lid, or by laying it across the mantel.

1 magnolia swag (includes 1 large bloom,
2 smaller blooms and 2 bud blooms)

2 rose picks with berries (2 rose blooms per stem)

3 pine sprays with cones

3 gold bell cups

3 stems of frosted and glittered grape ivy

pine spray with gold glitter, 30" (76cm)

7 gold twigs

gold papier-maché angel, 12" (30cm) tall

green moss

4 yards (365cm) of 3" (8cm) wide wired ribbon

10-light strand of holiday lights

green plastic floral candle holder, 3" (8cm) diameter

gold tray, 12" (30cm) diameter

pillar candle, 12" (30cm) tall, 3" (8cm) diameter

gold floral spray paint

green floral sheet foam, 2" (5cm) deep

floral adhesive tape

green floral tape

greening pins

wooden floral picks with wire

craft glue

This holiday arrangement sparkles # Holiday Angel & Candle Arrangement

with lots of gold and glitter, which looks so festive for the

holidays. Add a candle and holiday lights and this arrangement

radiates with soft light and elegance. This

particular design is done as a one-sided arrangement

project 15

because the angel is finished on only one side. Display it on your mantle, sofa table

or foyer side table.

90

PREPARE BASE TRAY

Cut two pieces of foam, the bottom foam 8" x 5" (20cm x 13cm), the top foam 3" x 5" (8cm x 13cm). Round off the corners of the foam with a knife. Put two 8" (20cm) strips of floral adhesive tape on the tray, and press the large bottom piece of foam securely on the tray. Put floral adhesive tape on top of the bottom foam piece and stack the smaller cut foam on top and off center to the right. Insert the floral candle holder in the center of the top foam block, pressing firmly.

3 INSERT ANGEL AND CANDLE

Insert the pillar candle in the holder, and insert the angel right next to it on the top foam block. Secure the angel with craft glue if it seems wobbly.

2 ADD MOSS

Cover the foam with moss, and secure it with greening pins.

4 ADD MAGNOLIA SWAG

Center the magnolia swag in front of the angel and candle on the top foam block. Fasten it with an extra wire stem bent in half. Add glue to secure the stem if necessary.

5 **PREPARE PINE SPRAYS**
Open up the branches of the three pine sprays. Using gold spray paint, lightly spray the pine stems with gold accents. Spray the cones more heavily with paint to make them stand out.

6 **ADD PINE SPRAYS**
Insert two pine sprays on either side of the arrangement into the bottom foam block. Insert the last spray in the front of the bottom foam, angled to the right.

7 **ADD ROSES**
Cut the rose picks to 15" to 20" (38cm to 51cm), then insert them on a diagonal with one stem pointing toward the back left side and the other toward the front right.

tip: If you plan to place this arrangement on a mantle or where the arrangement can hang down over a ledge, bend the pine and rose picks so they flow downward.

8 **ADD IVY**
Cut two 24" (61cm) ivy stems and one 12" (30cm) stem. Insert the two long stems on either side of the arrangement and the short stem in the front, underneath the center magnolia.

9 **ADD BELL CUPS**
Cut the stems of two medium bell cups to 6½" (17cm) and a small bell cup stem to 10" (25cm). Insert the medium bell cups in the front of the arrangement behind the center magnolia. Insert the small bell cup toward the base of the arrangement angled left of center.

10 **ADD BOWS**
Following the bow techniques on pages 83–84, use 3 yards (274cm) of ribbon to create a two-loop bow with 20" (51cm) streamers. Use 1 yard (91cm) of ribbon to create another two-loop bow with 10" (25cm) streamers. Insert the bows diagonally from each other with the smaller bow toward the back and the big bow at the base of the arrangement in the front left.

11 **ADD GLITTER PINE**
Cut two 20" (51cm) glittered pine stems and one 15" (38cm) stem. Insert the two long stems toward the back left of the arrangement with one just a touch higher than the other. Insert the short stem toward the front right of the arrangement.

12 **ADD GOLD TWIGS**
Cut one 22" (56cm) gold twig, four 18" (46cm) twigs and two 12" (30cm) twigs. Insert the longest twig within the glittered pine behind the angel. Insert the four 18" (46cm) twigs on either side and within the two rose picks. Insert the two shortest twigs toward the front left and right of center magnolia. If you cannot find gold twigs, just spray natural twigs with gold spray paint.

13 **ADD HOLIDAY LIGHTS**
Weave the holiday lights throughout the arrangement.

tip: I used the smallest light strand I could find because I wanted just enough light to make the gold accents glisten and to add a soft glow. Too many lights would overpower the arrangement.

14 **CREATE VARIATIONS**
To customize this arrangement so it can be displayed beyond the holiday season, substitute ivy for the evergreen. Change the figurine or replace it with another candle. Fill in the back of the arrangement like the front, and use it as a table centerpiece.

In addition to the mail-order and online resources listed here, check your local craft and floral supply shops for general floral tools and supplies. Purchase fine silk flowers from local craft stores or directly from your florist.

C.M. OFFRAY & SON, INC.
360 Route 24
Chester, NJ 07930
Phone: (800) 551-LION
www.offray.com
Decorative ribbons

DESIGN MASTER COLOR TOOL INC.
P.O. Box 601
Boulder, CO 80306
Phone: (303) 443-5214
Fax: (303) 443-5217
www.dmcolor.com
Floral color sprays, paints and tints

FLORACRAFT
One Longfellow Place
P.O. Box 400
Ludington, MI 49431
Phone: (616) 845-0240
www.floracraft.com
Floral sheet foam and general floral supplies

W.J. COWEE, INC.
28 Taylor Ave.
P.O. Box 248
Berlin, NY 12022
Phone: (800) 658-2233
Fax: (518) 658-2244
www.cowee.com
Wooden floral picks

Get Creative
WITH NORTH LIGHT BOOKS!

create your own

tabletop fountains

soothing
harmonious
elegant
simple

paris mannion

Now you can create your own tabletop fountains and add beautiful accents to your living room, bedroom, kitchen, garden and more. Author Paris Mannion gets you started with guidelines for making 15 gorgeous fountains using everything from lava rock and bamboo to shells and clay pots. Each project is detailed with step-by-step instructions and full color photos.

You'll learn to incorporate flowers, driftwood, fire, figurines, crystals, plants and more to personalize your fountains to create works of art that will have friends buzzing for years to come.
1-58180-103-3, paperback, 128 pages

Create your very own floral arrangements for priceless wedding memories with a personal touch. Terry Rye, a professional florist with twenty years of experience, will teach you step-by-step how to design more than 20 stunning floral arrangements. You'll find something for every part of your wedding—from the bride's bouquet to boutonnieres, from pew decorations to table centerpieces and wedding cake toppers.

Whether you are the bride-to-be, a member of the wedding party, a friend or an aspiring floral designer, this book will be your guide to easily creating beautiful wedding florals with striking results.
1-55870-560-0, paperback, 128 pages

Make your wedding elegant and unforgettable with these beautiful keepsake ideas. From the bridal veil to the guest book, this book provides you with 21 step-by-step projects that are fun, affordable and surprisingly easy to make. Best of all, you can complete each project using non-perishable materials, so everything can be finished well in advance of the big day.

Whether you're a bride, family member or friend, this guide will do more than show you how to create gorgeous wedding accessories—it will help bring your loved ones together to take part in this wonderful occasion.
1-55870-559-7, paperback, 128 pages

Discover a world of enchantment and creative possibilities with Sammie Crawford, The Fairy Gourdmother, and her painting and decorating techniques, patterns and practical instruction. It's easy—gourds are everywhere: in gardens, at the grocer or farmer's market. It's fun—whether you create a frog prince, a snowman, a lighthouse, or a bow-legged cowboy, you'll be smiling from start to finish. Includes eight step-by-step projects to show you how, plus plenty more examples to inspire you own ideas of what a gourd can be.
0-89134-993-6, paperback, 128 pages